How to Become a Life Coach

The Ultimate Guide to Becoming a Life Coach and Building a Successful Career in Life Coaching

by Vivian Sandau

Table of Contents

Introduction

If you're naturally gifted at dishing out advice to your friends, with words of inspiration and motivation, then life coaching may be your true calling. Life coaching has become a booming career field that can offer you significant monetary rewards, as well as plenty of opportunities to grow professionally. If you have the required traits, then it could be the perfect job for you. Furthermore, it offers a flexible schedule, as you can coach in person, on the phone, or online whenever it's convenient for you. In fact, you could create a successful career in life coaching, earning money from the comfort of your own home. Of course, before you get there, you'll need to know how to do it properly, and the path to success differs from one individual to another.

To determine whether you have the essential qualities necessary to become a life coach, let's do some self-assessment. Does your own life have direction? Are you good at talking to people and guiding them in making decisions about their lives? Do you enjoy spending time chatting with and listening to people? Do you have that sincere desire to lend a hand to people in need? Your answers to all of these questions ought to be in the affirmative for you to ultimately succeed in a life coaching career. The more you enjoy it, the better at it you'll become, and therefore the more successful you'll be. Can you envision yourself truly enjoying this line of work? If yes, then what are you waiting for? Let's get started!

Chapter 1: Life Coaching Basics

Believe it or not, even those with limited educational qualifications can become life coaches. For example, if you're a college undergraduate or if you never finished college, this career choice is not closed off to you by any means. That's because one of the perks of being a life coach is that it's self-regulated, and there are no specific educational requirements or professional licenses needed to start your career.

Life coaching is a relative newcomer as an officially recognized profession. Many people have been practicing life coaching for some time, but it was not recognized as a career until relatively recently. Nowadays, though, it not only has a specific job title, but it's expanding into several niches as well. You can create a specific niche of your own as you discover what your clients need the most.

What is life coaching?

Life coaching means helping people to utilize their full potential in setting goals and achieving them for a successful and happy life. Being a life coach, though, doesn't mean being a therapist or a counselor. So, you don't deal with the person's past, but instead you focus on his or her present and future. Some of the questions answered during life coaching are: "Where is the person now?" "What and where does he/she want to be in the future?"

As a life coach, your responsibility is to help the person find direction in their life. Your role is to guide them towards the correct path, based on their own goals and preferences. You're not there to dictate what goals and steps they should follow. You're only there to motivate and guide. This is because people have unique personalities. What's success to John may not be interpreted as success to Dave. Your major role is to help people realize their own desires and reach their full potential through their own efforts.

Consequently, if you are a professional therapist and/or a counselor, there's certainly no stopping you from becoming a life coach. This is the ideal package, because then you can use your training and experience to delve deep into the past and then help direct the person's future. But again, having been a professional therapist or counselor is not a requirement of becoming a life coach.

General types of coaching

1. **Personal** – This includes life, career, health, personal finance, wellness, weight loss, relationship and many more niches that involve personal development.

2. **Business** – This includes small businesses, marketing, internet based business, marketing and advertising, and similar niches.

Becoming a life coach is fantastic for people who sincerely love to be with people and help them succeed. Hence, if you're certain you can be this person then, by all means, go for it!

Chapter 2: How to Become a Life Coach

How can you become a life coach? It's easy! You let people know you're there to help them succeed; that you can help them attain their dreams and aspirations in life. You can conduct one-on-one coaching sessions or group consultations.

More specifically, here are the steps you can follow to become a life coach:

1. Find your Specific Niche

You can choose to be a life coach dealing with a specific niche, or a general life coach. There are advantages to selecting a niche, though. It's just like choosing a pediatrician for a sick child over a doctor without a specialization. People will be inclined to go to coaches who cater to their specific circumstances. You should choose the niche that you're most interested in. For example, choose relationship coaching if you're naturally inclined to help people succeed in their relationships; or choose career coaching if you're more comfortable helping people achieve their career goals.

2. Get a Business License

Life coaching is self-regulated but, if you want to establish your own business, you may need a business permit or business license. This will depend on the requirements of your state or district. Register your business with the institution required in your area. Talk to your lawyer about specific requirements, especially if you want to create a Corporation or LLC. Your lawyer can also assist you in preparing contracts or agreement documents between you and your clients. If you have a certification or degree, you can display it prominently in your office, or on your website. Setting aside a specific area for your office in your home is ideal, especially if you work predominantly online.

3. Create your Business Name, Logo, and Brand Slogan or Tagline

All businesses should have a name, logo and slogan. These will help in its advertisement. People will easily remember catchy names and logos. Create one that defines your goals and vision. Advertisers find red, blue, and yellow colors more eye-appealing to consumers, so choose one of these colors to include in your logo.

4. Set your Goals

This should be an easy step for you since setting goals is part of your expertise! As you know, a business without goals is a rudderless ship at sea, blown in all directions. It doesn't move forward because it can't. Your goals will determine your course of action. SMART goals are the most common and practical ways of setting your objectives. The goals should be S -- Specific; M -- Measurable; A – Attainable; R – relevant; and T – Time bound. This means your goals are stated in detail, are practical and have a specific timeframe in which they should be accomplished.

5. Advertise

Advertise your services online and offline. Advertising your services is essential for success. Your previous satisfied clients can become your advertisers through word-of-mouth, but this method is slow. You have to do some active marketing yourself, if you want to get your name out there. Here are various ways you can do that:

Online

- **Facebook** – Create a page on Facebook for your services and ask friends to like and share it. Post a link to your website or blog on your page.

- **Twitter** – Compose a 40-word catchy phrase and tweet it with a link to your website or blog.

- **LinkedIn** – Display your expertise, services, or website links on your LinkedIn page.

- **Pinterest** – Post an attractive photo of your services that users can share and comment on.

- **YouTube** – Create a video about your services and products. Use an image that can capture your viewers' interest as a thumbnail of the video.

- **Website** – This is ideal if you have also products such as eBooks, books, journals and instructional videos to market. You can display them all on your website and let clients buy and/or contact you online. If you don't want to pay somebody else to create your website, then try making it yourself using SquareSpace or Wix – these are very easy do-it-yourself website creators that are inexpensive and self-explanatory.

- **Blog** – This can serve as an extension of your website, where you can post related articles and clients can interact with you through comments or live chat applications.

- **Email** – You can also send the details of your services through emails. Remember to include your contact information.

- **Life Coach Associations** – Enlist your name in related organizations such as the International Coach Federation (ICF). If there are life coaching groups in your state then you can register with them as well.

- **Online yellow pages** – Check whether your name and services are included in the online yellow pages.

- **Prepare free tutorials** – If you're still starting, you can prepare tutorial programs and offer them for free in your website.

- **Craigslist** – This is one of the most popular websites that you can enlist your services on, for free. More and more people are using Craigslist to search for services and products.

- **Guest posts** – Write guest posts as a life coach and publish them on popular blogs. Include a link to your website in the author's page.

- **LivePerson** – You could have an entire life coaching career on this website. Clients can find you here, and you'll be able to chat with them or speak with them over the phone, and you'll be paid directly through the website.

Offline

- **Radio** – This method is the perfect way to target people who are constantly on the road.

- **TV** – This is expensive but can be more effective than radio and news because it uses motion, graphics and texts.

- **Local Newspapers** – This is an effective method for people who prefer to read rather than watch TV, or listen to the radio.

- **Magazines** – This provides more visual presentation and graphics but is more expensive than newspapers.

- **Flyers** – This is practical and cheap. You can prepare the flyers yourself using your computer and printer, and post them in local spots where you envision your clients frequenting, such as coffee shops, grocery stores, etc.

- **Business cards** – You can order business cards by the bulk. Include your logo and contact information. Vistaprint is one of the most popular and least expensive companies to order business cards from, and you can design them right on their website as well.

- **Telephone directory** – Many people still use the phone directory to search for services. Get them as your clients.

- **Posters** – Posters that are well prepared are superb advertising materials. You should post them in busy areas.

- **Events** – Talk to the event planners to see whether you can display your services. You may be asked to pay a fee but, if you're lucky, you may be able advertise for free. At the very least, you can spread the word by mingling with other people at the event.

- **Trade Fairs** – You can rent a booth or a stall to display your life coaching materials and let your community know about your services.

- **Conduct seminars** – You can conduct seminars or give speeches about life coaching in different venues. You can offer it for free as long as they prepare the venue and the audience for you. This is a great way to advertise and invite people to be your clients. Distribute your business cards and other necessary materials after the seminar.

6. Keep in Touch with your Clients

Your life coaching clients are your clients forever. If you have coached your first clients well, they'll remain yours for as long as they live. Getting the first client is often the toughest part, but once you've gotten your first one, the next will not be so difficult. As with any business, it can take months or years to establish a steady stream of income from life coaching. Don't get discouraged though, your effort and determination will eventually pay off with big rewards.

Chapter 3: Establishing a Successful Career as a Professional Life Coach

Establishing a successful career as a life coach is like providing a compass and a map for a ship captain. You can only be successful if your client succeeds as well. In this example, the captain is your client, and you're the map and compass. Hence, before the journey has started, the captain must know where he wants to go, and your role is to help him get there. He must be willing to be coached and be willing to be the main proponent of the journey. You're there primarily to guide, motivate, and help him recognize his own goals and develop the potential necessary to learn to design his own goals and succeed in achieving them.

After you have implemented the steps found in chapter 2, you should strive not merely to be a life coach, but to be a successful one. To establish a successful career in life coaching, you need to be aware that there's no single formula for success. You'll have to discover what can work for you as you gain more experience. The following are methods you can adapt to assist you in your quest.

1. Educate Yourself Continually

Although you don't need a college degree or certification to become a life coach, you have to find a way to acquire more information about life coaching and life coaching techniques. Advance your education by enrolling in online courses. You can also enroll in related post-graduate courses such as psychology, guidance counseling or other behavioral courses that can enhance your life coaching skills.

This can give you the opportunity to be a therapist, counselor and life coach, all at the same time, thereby, increasing your professional value. This is because clients you don't personally know may choose someone with higher educational qualifications, or someone who has some certificate to show. Enhancing what you know will also increase the scope of what you can do.

Additionally, while advancing your education, you can simultaneously develop your skills in the following areas:

- **Establishing trust** – You can only establish trust if you prove yourself to be trustworthy. How? By being honest, sincere, and straightforward with your clients.

- **Listening** – A good communicator is a good listener. Listen and understand what your client is telling you.

- **Motivating** – You have to learn how to initiate your client's actions. Provide him with enough stimuli to start acting on his goals. You can do this by citing the rewards he can gain if he's able to meet his goals.

- **Questioning** – Learn how to ask the right questions. You can base your questions on the client's previous statements.

- **Preparing goals** – Be aware that goals can be short-term or long-term. Your goals during the sessions are usually short term goals because you have to constantly assess the validity of your client's action plan. This is the only way you can re-direct his course of action if the plan doesn't work for him.

- **Managing problems** – There are various ways to manage or solve a problem. Present them as challenges to your client so that he'll be glad to tackle them. If there are problems with the process itself, learn how to resolve it. Experience is the best teacher. It doesn't need to be your own, though. You can learn from the experiences of other coaches too.

- **Assessing of results** – Know how to assess results accurately. Do this by designing the action plan in such a way that it includes a category "done" "or not done." The checklist will clearly provide you the correct information, whether the action plan was completed satisfactorily or not.

- **Redirecting** – Learn how to redirect the course of action by using flow charts and providing at least two alternatives, should the first action plan prove unsuccessful.

2. Undergo training

Undergoing training on a reliable program will definitely increase your chances of being hired. Online courses and training designed for life coaching have recently become available, which you can easily avail yourself of. Certificates will be issued after the training. So, if anyone asks you whether you have any certification, you can proudly show them your certificate. Clients tend to choose a life coach who has proof of their training.

You ought to attend life coaching seminars and lectures too. You should aim to attend any and every event that could enrich your career, especially those that are free or aren't out of your budget.

3. Train with an expert

Learn from the best. This is another effective option you can choose. Volunteer as an assistant to a life coach who has extensive exposure, and learn from him. Observe him closely and pay attention to how he interviews, designs plans and motivate clients. Your observations will serve as pointers for you. Nevertheless, you have to create your own style that you are most comfortable with.

4. Practice, practice, practice

It takes persistent practice and constant exposure to excel in your career. Practice makes perfect. Activities such as interviewing, motivating, communicating and asking questions are skills, which can only be perfected through practice. Hence, ask for the support of your family and friends so that you can hone your skills.

Chapter 4: How to Practice Life Coaching

How do you actually "do" life coaching? Do you just start interviewing the client and then map a course of action for him? Before you initiate any action, you must remember that the client is the major participant in this activity, and you're only playing a supporting role. You don't dictate what he should do; you guide him and motivate him to do what he wants. You can do this through the following techniques.

Step #1 – Your client contacts you or vice-versa

If you don't know your client personally, you can get to know him first by offering a free session to do so. When the client decides to continue with your services, you draw an agreement and he pays for the succeeding sessions. He can also pay each time he comes for his sessions. You must have a variety of payment schemes, so that your clients can select what's convenient for them.

Moreover, you should prepare a welcome kit to guide your client about the details of your services. You can include small gift items such as key chains with your logo and similar items, and any informational pamphlets that explain your process.

You can do the session online using video cams or web chats, or you can go offline with a person-to-person meet up. This depends upon your set-up, the circumstances surrounding the process, your client-coach agreement and what you have advertised.

Step #2 – Conduct the first session

This is the official start of your life coaching with your client. Ascertain that all agreements are properly signed and noted. Explain the process clearly to your client. It should be clear in your agreement that you're not his doctor or therapist, so anything concerning his health must be referred to his doctor. You can conduct your coaching sessions for 30 minutes or one hour, once or twice a week for 3 to 4 months. This will depend upon the need of your client.

Furthermore, he needs to know that all decisions are his responsibility. He has to commit himself completely to the activity because his success will depend upon his active participation. The following are the activities that you have to accomplish during the first session.

Talk to your client

In this phase, you proceed further in having a heart-to-heart talk with your client. Be a smart communicator by listening more and talking less. Allow your client to express what he wants to do in his life and what he wants to achieve. What is his perception of success? What does being self-fulfilled to him mean? Different people perceive success in different ways, so be careful in treading through this path. Let him reveal what he wants in his life, in his own way.

Observe verbal and non-verbal cues. What does his body language say about his real thoughts? He might be saying something that his actions contradict. Some negative non-verbal signs are: crossing the arms, avoiding eye contact, physically distancing himself from you, and fidgeting.

In cases when you feel the client is rejecting you through his non-verbal language, you have take a step back and first establish trust. Your client must trust you before he can relax and express himself openly. Only when he does this will you be able to create goals for him. Start by asking positive questions about his dreams, his hobbies and the things that fire him up. Make him feel that you're sincerely interested in him as a person.

Ask leading questions

After the client relaxes and is reassured that you're there to help him out, you can start asking significant questions. Ask leading questions to clarify what the client wants to achieve. Probe deeper by asking the questions that might lead your client in the right direction.

When clarifying, you can say: "You have stated that ... What do you mean by your statement?" You can also let him define what success means to him. "You mean if you do that, you'll be successful?" Your questions should not appear rude or extremely inquisitive. Don't talk down to your client, instead talk to him as an equal. You may be the expert, but it's his life on the line, he's the boss. Have a meaningful conversation with him.

Establish his goals for a specific time (at least 3 goals)

Based on your conversation, establish your client's goals or objectives. As mentioned previously, the most popular way of establishing goals is to make use of the SMART method. Your client must be the major planner. Let him be the one to decide which ones will be his final goals.

This is where your motivational skills come in. Through your client's notion of success, ask him what he thinks he should do to attain success. From this, you can clarify steps for him to undertake, with a designated timetable. The goals should be created in such a way that he can also monitor his progress. This way he will feel empowered and know that his success depends solely on him. It's his plan, so he will be committed towards the achievement of the goals that he has personally set.

Let your client prepare 3-5 goals, and prepare his action plan. His action plan must be specific and easy to follow.

Step #3 – Assess the previous goals to determine whether they were attained

Your client comes back for another scheduled session. This is the phase where you assess your client's progress. Through the SMART goals, you can evaluate accurately what your client has accomplished. Your client should be familiar with the designated time frame in which he ought to fulfill the tasks. Pay attention to the fact that these are his goals and his course of action, so he should take full responsibility and stick religiously to the plan.

This doesn't mean, though, that plans can't be redirected during the course of implementation. If the railroad ahead is broken, then he doesn't have any alternative but to change direction. That's why it's important that there be alternative plans that he can utilize in case this happens.

Step #4 – Set up the next course of action from the assessment results

What course of action worked and what did not? What goals were achieved and what were not? Are the outcomes as expected? Discuss with your client the rationale behind the failures and the successes. From these, you can create the next action plan. The number of sessions will depend upon your client.

Step #5 – Terminate your services

After your client's goals have been achieved, you're now ready to terminate your services. Wait for the client to initiate this phase. He may opt to go on with your services. In this case, you will have to help the client to set new goals again. If both of you agreed on terminating the contract, ascertain that your client has your contact information or business card. That way, he can easily contact you in case he needs your services, or if any of his family members and friends require your expertise.

Chapter 5: Guide to a Successful Life Coaching

Accomplishing all that has been mentioned so far doesn't ensure success if you don't follow this guide. These guidelines will increase your chances of succeeding. Successful life coaching depends on several factors, namely your attitude and that of your clients; your communication skills; your related traits and personality; your experience; and your educational background.

Attitude counts

A positive attitude attracts positive reactions. When you're optimistic, you have a cheerful demeanor. You believe that there are no problems you can't solve. In this way you inspire trust and respect. Develop traits such as honesty, sincerity, promptness, empathy, calmness, loyalty, resourcefulness, and all the positive traits you can assimilate. These are all necessary assets when you go out and practice your profession.

Your client's attitude also counts. Your client must be willing to be coached. He must be open to suggestions and new ideas. He should be motivated to take charge of his life. You can help him with this aspect through proper motivation.

Communication skills are essential

Your communication skills are vital in your career. Without them, you won't be able to let your client open up about his fears, aspirations and feelings. Some naturally acquire this skill because of their amiable personality, but don't fret if you don't have it. It can be cultivated. You can practice your skills with your family members and trusted friends.

Practice what you preach

You can't inspire others if your life is in shambles. Your life is still in progress but it should reflect positivity that your client can emulate. You will be more credible if you practice what you preach. Organize your own life to serve as a good example to your clients. Show them that you have imperfections, just like anyone else, but that you strive to overcome them. When the client sees this in you, he'll be inspired and motivated to follow your footsteps.

Deal with the present and the future of your client

Unless you're a therapist and a counselor, you can't and shouldn't delve deeper into your client's past life. Remember to concentrate on what and where he is now, and to where he wants to be. Your client has to be aware of this too, so that you'll be on the same page when planning for his goals. You can suggest or recommend based on your experience but he has to have the final say. Your client must understand that coaching is a self-help process.

Chapter 6: 25 Key Life Coaching Tips

You can start small with your life coaching career, but you can go big time by remembering these 25 key tips:

1. **Organize your workflow**. You can facilitate your work load if you have a flow chart that designates how the work ought to proceed. This flow chart will help a lot when you start hiring assistants or more personnel.

2. **Utilize all advertising methods available**. Advertising is crucial to putting you on your clients' map. Use all the methods mentioned in chapter 2 to maximize your exposure. When done correctly, you'll have clients knocking at your door in no time at all.

3. **Ensure that all your related documents are in order**. Your certificates and diplomas (if any) should be displayed prominently in your office. Your contract or agreement with your client must be prepared properly. Your business permit must also be in order. A lawyer can help with this aspect.

4. **Maximize your earning capabilities**. You can earn through various methods such as personal or group coaching; sale of self-authored books or newsletters; conducting seminars and lectures; and developing life coaching software.

5. **Choose a specific niche**. It's best to choose a specific niche and specialize in it. You can add other niches as you gain more experience.

6. **Align yourself with appropriate organizations.** This is a perfect method for enlisting yourself in life coaching organizations. It means you belong to the group. If a client searches for you online, your name will easily pop up.

7. **Continue educating yourself.** Education is a lifelong process. Keep learning new information. Update yourself with new methodologies. Acquire certification and more training. If possible, pursue a masters or doctorate degree.

8. **Coaching is a two way process.** You and your client must work together for your client to attain success. You suggest and recommend based on his ideas and preferences, and he makes the final decision.

9. **Have a positive outlook.** View your client's thought processes positively. Don't say: "That's not possible," or "That can never happen," instead say: "That can be done," or "Let's make it happen."

10. **Challenge people to do their best.** Challenge your client to give his best by providing him examples of how common people succeeded. Say: "If they can, why can't you?"

11. **Inspire through example.** Show them that the process works for you too. Teach by example.

12. **Be consistent.** Be consistent in what you're trying to impart to your client. If you have said something already, don't go back on it. Consistency encourages your client to feel secure and settled.

13. **Be trustworthy.** Your client's revelations are for your ears only. Whatever is disclosed during the life coaching sessions has to remain within the room's four corners. There's an increased rate of success if your clients trust you.

14. **Be honest.** Honesty is still the best policy. When you're honest with your client, plans and goals will be more accurate and reliable. Informing your client honestly that you don't know the answer to one of his questions will make him admire you more. You can say: "I don't know the answer to your question right now, but I'll do some research and provide you with the answer in our next session."

15. Be reliable. You're reliable if you have offered effective and accurate services. This indicates that your methods are successful.

16. Motivate your client internally. You have to motivate your client in such a way that he becomes self-motivated. His actions must come from a sincere desire to succeed.

17. Learn how to empathize with your client. You must empathize with your client to understand him more. How does it feel to be in his shoes? How would you feel if you were in his place?

18. Have the sincere desire to help. Do life coaching primarily because you sincerely want to help people, and not because of the monetary rewards. The money is obviously important, but you should know what your priorities are. Foremost has to be people. This sincere desire will reflect on the way you conduct your coaching sessions, and on the way you treat your clients. When clients notice this, they'll trust you more and will seek only your services.

19. Observe professional conduct. Be a professional at all times. Professionals don't go into temper tantrums, use profane language, throw fits, gossip about clients, and charge exorbitant fees. No matter what the client's attitude is, as a professional, you should always stay calm and collected.

20. **Build good relationships with your clients.** Your relationship with your clients can determine whether they'll continue hiring you or not. Be friendly, warm and approachable.

21. **Make sure your client feels responsible for the outcome**. Always remind your client that whatever outcomes the process yields will be his responsibility. Let him own the process. It's his goals and his plans; you just guide and direct him through the process.

22. **Draw out the client's potential to design his own goals**. You don't dictate. Just as your client is responsible for the outcomes, he should also be responsible for designing his own goals. This is done through your motivation and guidance. It's only when he does this that he will feel that he indeed does play the major role in the activity.

23. **Enabling and empowering your client to attain success in his life is your primary goal.** You're coaching your client to succeed in his life by enabling and empowering him. You're not there to get him do what you think is right for him. You're there to clarify and guide him to what he believes is best for him. Of course, there are exceptions to this rule, so look out for those exceptions.

24. Have an evaluation form ready for the client. This is to determine the effectiveness and reliability of your services. After the coaching sessions, you can allow your client to evaluate your services. This will give you accurate information about its strengths and weaknesses.

25. Conclude your sessions properly. Your culminating session has to end properly. A Termination of Contract should be signed by both parties. You may want to provide brochures or business cards for his friends, coupled with a parting gift for him. Congratulate the client for a task well done and give him important reminders to maintain his success.

Refer to these pointers whenever you conduct a life coaching activity and you'll increase your chances of succeeding. Remember, it's not all about you, but it's all about your client.

Chapter 7: Taking it to the Next Level by Enrolling in an 8-Week Training & Certification Course

If you've read everything in this book up to this point, then give yourself a big pat on the back. You're clearly quite serious about pursuing this career path – and for good reason since it has so much to offer!

You may consider next enrolling in an 8-week training and certification seminar online, which can take you from being a pretty good life coach to becoming a life-changing and money-making life coach.

Here are just some of the things you'll learn:

- **The Value Creation System** – Here you will learn the exact steps needed to make your services so valuable that no one will be able to resist your offer.

- **Level One Coaching Model** – Learn the first steps involved in creating a simple but effective model of coaching that will enable you to help others reach new levels of potential.

- **Entrepreneurial and Small Business Coaching** – Here I'll show you how to coach those natural born entrepreneurs who run their own business so they can maximize their profits.

- **Career Planning and Development Coaching** – Learn the difference between coaching those interested in taking their career to next level vs. those who work for themselves and how you can help them get ahead in their profession.

- **Artistic Creativity Coaching** – In this part of the program, you will learn how to help natural born artists take their talents and abilities to the next level so they can gain the most fulfillment possible.

- **Identifying The Perfect Candidate** – Here you'll learn how to pick the right type of candidate based on the type of coaching needed to help them excel.

- **Emotional Mastery** – Because emotions are what ultimately drive our behaviors, you will learn how to motivate others to take action by effectively tapping into their emotions and becoming a master of influence.

- **Goal Setting** – Every person needs to set goals to achieve success. Here I'll show you a simple but effective system for getting anyone to set measurable and realistic goals.

- **Relationship Development** - your ability to build and sustain relationships is ultimately what is going to enable you to be successful as a life coach. In this part of the program I'll teach you everything you've ever wanted to know about developing powerful relationships with your clients that will last a lifetime.

- **Communication Tactics** - Not everyone processes information the same way and because of that you need to be able to communicate with each client differently. Here I'll share some special techniques that will enable you to understand the best method of communication for each particular client

- **Assessing Needs** - After understanding what your clients ultimate goals are in life, you will now be able to understand how to accurately assess their needs based on what they want to achieve. It may sound simple but in reality, sometimes people don't even realize their own needs.

- **The Power of Questions** - In this part of the program you'll learn how to utilize questions to extract the information that you need to take your client to the next level.

- **Mastering Intuition** - within all of us is a voice guiding us to the right direction. Sometimes however, it can be challenging to see her or trust that voice. Here you'll not only learn to identify your own intuition, but you'll learn how to teach others to identify it as well.

- **Preparing For The Role** - even if you have no idea how a life coach should present him or herself, don't worry, because in this part of the program, I'll show you exactly what clients expect from a life coach and how to deliver it .

- **Motivational Tactics** – Here, I'll reveal a simple but effective method to instantly inspire and motivate your client to take action and strive for success.

- **Developing Rapport** -sometimes helping a person maximize their potential involves tough conversations. In order to have those conversations, you're going to have to develop the right rapport with your client. In this part of the program, I'll show you exactly how to do that.

- **Four Circles of The Coaching** Model - In this part of the program, you'll be introduced to the four circles of the coaching model, which will give you a telescopic view of how the whole system works.

- **Your First Consultation** - Here I'll show you the exact steps to take during your first consultation so that it goes smooth and sets the pace for future coaching sessions.

- **Honing Your Approach Technique** - In this part of the program I'll show you how to begin to develop the technique that you will use in your approach to help lead your client to success.

- **Overcoming Setbacks** - just because you set the direction for your client doesn't necessarily mean that they will never experience challenges and setbacks. It is your ability to overcome those aspects of the game that will ultimately enable you to gain their respect. You'll learn everything you need to know about doing so in this part of the program.

- **Program Development** - Here you'll learn how to assess your clients' goals and put together a program for them to follow so that their dreams don't fall by the wayside.

- **Confronting Hesitation** - Not every client is going to be ready to be proactive and take action. Here you'll learn how to get even the most unmotivated person ready to take charge of their life.

- **Developing Homework Assignments** - Here I'll show you a step-by-step system that will enable you to give your client home work assignments that will ensure they are staying on track to achieve their goals.

- **And much much more!**

If you're feeling proactive and ready to get started right away, simply open the below link in a web browser. The additional information you need will be at your fingertips!

Go to this link: http://bit.ly/ZKcbFB

Conclusion

Life coaching is an excellent career choice if this is what you feel inspired to do, and to be successful, you'll have to discover the correct formula that fits your personality and preferences. Life coaching provides a genuine opportunity to help people make more of their lives. It also offers superb opportunities for self-advancement, both financially and professionally. In addition, you can start small, with no certification or college education at all, and then slowly enhance your skills as you prosper. You can always pursue further education or acquire certification as you go along.

Although, life coaching doesn't require a license in the states, you should still strive for a life coaching certification to fully develop your skills. Don't rest on your laurels. If you find success with your first clients, strive to further improve your services. Use the steps, recommendations and guidelines presented here and you won't go astray.

If you believe you have the traits necessary to become a life coach, then take hold of this opportunity and go for it! This is your chance to help people achieve their dreams in life, while fulfilling your own at the same time. What could be more rewarding?

Last, I'd like to thank you for purchasing this book! If you enjoyed it or found it helpful, I'd greatly appreciate it if you'd take a moment to leave a review on Amazon. Thank you, and Good Luck!

Made in United States
Orlando, FL
01 May 2024

46385524R00033